How Did We
Find Out About
THE ATMOSPHERE?

The "HOW DID WE FIND OUT . . . ?" SERIES,
by Isaac Asimov

HOW DID WE FIND OUT—

The Earth Is Round?
About Electricity?
About Numbers?
About Dinosaurs?
About Germs?
About Vitamins?
About Comets?
About Energy?
About Atoms?
About Nuclear Power?
About Outer Space?
About Earthquakes?
About Black Holes?
About Our Human Roots?
About Antarctica?
About Oil?
About Coal?
About Solar Power?
About Volcanoes?
About Life in the Deep Sea?
About the Beginning of Life?
About the Universe?
About Genes?
About Computers?
About Robots?
About the Atmosphere?

How Did We
Find Out About
THE ATMOSPHERE?

Isaac Asimov

Illustrated by David Wool

Walker and Company
New York

First published in the United States of America
in 1985 by the Walker Publishing Company, Inc.

Published simultaneously in Canada by John Wiley & Sons
Canada, Limited, Rexdale, Ontario.

Library of Congress Cataloging in Publication Data

Asimov, Isaac, 1920–
    How did we find out about the atmosphere?

    (How did we find out—series)
    Summary: Traces the history of the scientific discovery of "atmo-
sphere" and its properties.
    1. Atmosphere—Juvenile literature. [1. Atmosphere]
I. Wool, David, ill. II. Title. III. Series: Asimov,
Isaac, 1920–   . How did we find out—series.
QC863.5.A85 1985   551.5'09   84-27125
ISBN 0-8027-6580-7 (Reinf.)
ISBN 0-8027-6588-2 (Trade)

Printed in the United States of America

10 9 8 7 6 5 4 3 2 1

Dedicated to:
Mary Allerton C. Fiske,
who keeps things going.

Contents

A Tornado

1 Atoms and Pressure

THE AIR THAT surrounds us and the whole Earth is called the "atmosphere" (AT-moh-sfeer), which comes from Greek words meaning "ball of air."

Usually we pay little attention to the air. We can't see it or feel it. It seems to be nothing at all. If we open a box and it contains only air, we say, "It's empty. There's nothing in it."

Just the same we know that air exists. When I say we can't feel it, I mean we can't feel the air when it is *still*. The Sun heats the air, however, and in some places it is heated more than in others. Warm air rises and cool air moves in to take its place. This moving air is called "wind."

We can feel the wind against our face and body. It makes us uncomfortable in winter, for the winter wind carries warmth away from our body and makes us feel much colder. In the summer, though, a wind can be pleasant for it cools us off.

When the wind is very strong, we don't like it at any time for it can do much damage. Hurricanes and tornados are examples of winds that move so fast they can knock down trees and destroy houses. Anyone who has ever experienced such storms doesn't think that air is "nothing."

The ancients knew that air was something, even if it was invisible, for the same reasons we do. The Greek philosopher Anaximenes (AN-ak-SIM-ih-neez, 570–500 B.C.) thought air was the basic material out of which all other substances were formed.

Not everyone agreed with him. A later philosopher, Empedocles (em-PED-uh-kleez, 492–432 B.C.), thought air was important but that the Earth was built of four basic substances: earth, water, and fire, in addition to air. This notion of the four basic substances lasted for two thousand years.

Air is different, in some ways, from other substances. You can see water and all the different things of the earth—rocks, sand, trees, animals, plants. You can even see fire. You can't see air, however. Does it really exist? The wind exists, of course, but maybe that's something different. When there's no wind, maybe there's nothing at all there.

The first person to show that even still air *is* something was a Greek engineer, Hero, who did his work about A.D. 50. (We don't know the exact dates of his birth and death.)

Hero pointed out that if you upended a container and put it into water, opening down, the water did not enter the container. That was because it was full of air, so there was no room for the water. If you made a hole in the bottom of the container, so that air could bubble out, then water would enter.

Another odd thing about air that Hero discovered

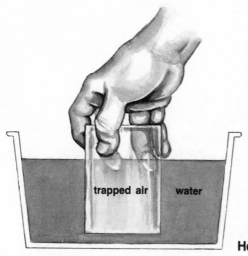

Hero's air experiment

was that it didn't seem to have much weight, if any. If you fill a container with sand or water, it becomes heavier and harder to lift. If you fill a balloon with air, on the other hand, it doesn't feel any heavier than an empty balloon.

Hero's answer to that depended on the work of an earlier Greek philosopher, Democritus (deh-MOK-rih-tus, 470–380 B.C.). Democritus had thought that everything was composed of particles far too small to see. These particles could not be broken up into anything smaller, he thought, so he called them "atoms" (A-tomz) from a Greek word meaning "unbreakable."

Democritus couldn't get most other philosophers to believe him, but a few did. Hero believed that atoms existed. He felt that in things that were solid or liquid, the atoms touched each other. In any quantity of these substances, there would be many, many atoms and their tiny weights would add up so that sand and water were heavy. In air, the atoms were spaced very widely

Robert Boyle's experiment

apart. A quantity of air contains very few atoms for that reason and that is why air doesn't seem to have weight in the way that sand and water do.

Then, too, since substances like sand and water have their atoms in contact, you can't squeeze those atoms closer together. You can't make sand or water take up less room than they do. In other words you can't "compress" sand or water—or other solids or liquids, either.

Hero pointed out that air *could* be compressed. It could be squeezed into a smaller volume, because the far-apart atoms could be forced to move closer together.

No one paid any more attention to Hero than they did to Democritus. As the centuries passed, however, there were always a few people who wondered if perhaps atoms existed. In 1662, a British scientist, Robert Boyle, took up the matter.

He used a seventeen-foot tube shaped like a J, opened at the long end and closed at the short. He added mercury, which filled the bottom of the J and trapped some air in the short end. The more mercury he added, the more the weight of mercury squeezed the trapped air into taking up less and less room. Hero was right.

Boyle also didn't accept the old Greek notion of four basic substances. He felt that the correct way of telling whether something was a basic substance, or "element" (EL-eh-ment), was to see whether it could be changed into something simpler. Only a substance that could *not* be changed into anything simpler was an element.

To most people it seemed that air was still an

element even from Boyle's viewpoint.

Beginning in 1803, the world of science began to accept atoms and, eventually, no one doubted their existence. Nowadays, we know that atoms usually cling together in small groups called "molecules" (MOL-uh-kyoolz), which comes from a Latin word meaning "a small body."

Of course, if air consisted of molecules it had to have some weight. The molecules were spread widely apart so a quantity of air wouldn't weigh much, but it would weigh *something*. In 1643, this thought occurred to the Italian scientist Evangelista Torricelli (tor-righ-CHEL-lee, 1608–1647).

He was considering the pumping of water. You can pump water to a height of four hundred inches above its original level. No amount of working the pump could force the water higher than that.

Torricelli thought that perhaps water could be pumped because the weight of the air pushed it upward. Perhaps the total weight of a column of air, resting on the water, was only enough to support a column of water four hundred inches high and no more.

One way of testing this would be to use mercury. Mercury is a heavy liquid, 13.4 times as dense as water; that is, a column of mercury an inch across and thirty inches high would weigh just as much as a column of water an inch across and four hundred inches high.

Torricelli took a four-foot-long tube closed at one end, filled it with mercury, and corked it. He upended it into a large dish of mercury and removed the cork. The mercury did not pour out entirely. A column of

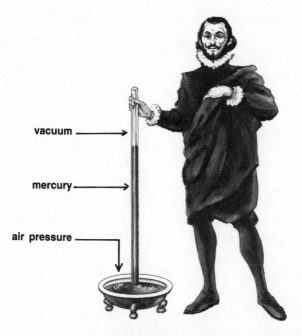

vacuum

mercury

air pressure

Torricelli's first barometer—1643

mercury thirty inches high remained in the tube held up by the weight of air.

The weight of the air on a particular bit of surface is called "air pressure." Air pressure must be nearly fifteen pounds per square inch to hold up thirty inches of mercury or four hundred inches of water.

It seems a little puzzling that there should be so much weight resting on every bit of your body without you feeling it. Air pressure, however, pushes in every direction on your body, and your body is filled with gas and liquid that pushes back with the very same pressure. In that way, you end up feeling nothing at all.

Torricelli's column of mercury which measures the air pressure is now called a "barometer." The weight of a particular portion of the atmosphere varies slightly from moment to moment. By noting whether the barometer is high or low, rising or falling, it is possible to predict the weather.

Torricelli's experiment proved something important. The ancients had believed that air filled all of space right up to the Moon and other heavenly bodies.

If, however, there was that much air above us, it would weigh much more than it does. If the air was the same density all the way up, then in order to have a pressure of fifteen pounds per square inch, it could only be five miles deep.

On the other hand, if you went high in the air, the air pressure would drop because much of the air would then be below you. It would only be the portion above you that would weigh down upon you, and that would be less and less as you went higher and higher.

The French scientist Blaise Pascal (pas-KAL, 1623–1662) sent his brother-in-law up a mountain in France with two barometers. Sure enough, the level of the mercury column dropped lower and lower as he went higher and higher.

The atmosphere doesn't stay at the same density as you go higher. The very bottom of the atmosphere has to bear all the weight of the miles of air above. That weight compresses the lowermost layer. As one goes upward, there is less and less weight of air above, so that that air is less compressed.

As you go higher, then, the air gets less and less dense; that is, the molecules of air move farther and farther apart, and a given weight of air takes up more and more room. For that reason, it was soon realized that the air must extend higher than five miles. That doesn't mean it weighs more; it just takes up more room.

Finally, of course, the air thins out till it is just about empty space, with only an occasional atom here and there. Such emptiness is a "vacuum" (VAK-yoom) from a Greek word for "empty." The vacuum extends all the way to the Moon and beyond it to the farthest star. It is only because of the thin layer of atmosphere around the Earth, that living things like ourselves can live.

2 Gases

IF WATER IS allowed to stand in an open container, it slowly dries up. What happens to it? Does it disappear into nothing?

Actually, the tiny molecules that make up water move into the air, bit by bit, and separate widely, forming a "vapor" (VAY-per), which comes from a Latin word for "steam." This vapor rises high in the air, and in the cold, forms little droplets of water again. If there are enough such droplets, we see them as clouds. Eventually, the water comes back to Earth as rain. The water vapor that forms when water dries, or "evaporates" (ee-VAP-oh-rates), is like air in its properties.

Other liquids, such as alcohol and turpentine, can also evaporate to form vapors. Liquids do so more rapidly when they are heated. When the vapors are cooled, they turn into liquids again.

Of course, air seems different since it doesn't turn to liquid on even the coldest winter days, even in Antarctica.

About 1520, the Belgian chemist Jan Baptista van Helmont (van-HEL-mont, 1580–1644) became interested in vapors. He observed that solids and liquids always had a certain volume, but vapors did not. If you put a quantity of sand or water into a large container, they filled only part of the container. *A vapor fills all of it, no matter how large the container.*

The water cycle

Vapors (and air, too) seemed to Helmont to be jumbled-up substances compared to the more orderly liquids and solids.

The ancient Greeks thought that the universe was developed from a primitive sort of matter that was all jumbled up. They called this primitive matter "chaos" (KAY-os). Van Helmont thought vapors and air were very much like the original chaos, and that's what he called them. However, he said the word as he pronounced it in his own language and it came out "gas."

Eventually, the word was adopted by everyone. We now think of air, and all vapors, as examples of "gases."

Van Helmont isolated a gas from burning wood which he called "gas sylvestre," meaning "gas from wood." It was not quite a vapor because it didn't change into a liquid when it was cooled. Nor was it air, either, because it didn't seem to behave exactly like air.

Van Helmont's work didn't make a big splash, but in 1756, the Scottish chemist Joseph Black (1728–1799) found that if he heated the mineral limestone, it turned into another substance—lime. In the process a gas was released which Black studied carefully. This gas, it turned out eventually, was the same as van Helmont's. Nowadays the gas is called "carbon dioxide" (KAHR-bon-dy-OK-side).

If carbon dioxide is placed in contact with lime, the lime will slowly turn back into limestone. Oddly enough, if lime is allowed to stand in pure air without contact with carbon dioxide, it also will turn back into limestone, though very slowly.

From this Black concluded that air contains a small amount of carbon dioxide as part of its structure.

This was the first indication that air is not a simple, uniform substance, as an element ought to be. It is a mixture of gases, for it contains carbon dioxide. Of course, it doesn't contain much, for only 0.035 percent (about 1/3,000) of the volume of the air is carbon dioxide.

Black found that the breath exhaled by people contained more carbon dioxide than ordinary air did. At least, exhaled breath turned lime into limestone faster than air did. When a candle burned, it produced carbon dioxide also.

One important way in which carbon dioxide differs from ordinary air, Black discovered, was that a candle would burn in air but not in carbon dioxide. Black tried to burn a candle in a closed container of air. The candle went out long before the wax was completely consumed. Black wasn't surprised because if the candle produced carbon dioxide, there would finally be enough of that gas in the closed container to smother the flame.

Black then removed the carbon dioxide from the closed container by adding lime. That left plenty of air in the container, air that was not carbon dioxide. Just the same, the candle wouldn't burn in the air after the carbon dioxide had been removed.

Black was puzzled and handed the problem over to a student of his, the Scottish chemist Daniel Rutherford (1749–1819). In 1772, Rutherford repeated Black's experiment with great care and in more detail. He made sure that all the carbon dioxide was removed, and he also ended up with a gas that was not quite air for it would not support a flame.

At this time, chemists were working with a theory of combustion that involved a substance they called "phlogiston" (floh-JIS-ton), which comes from a Greek word meaning "to burn." According to the theory, when something burned the burning material transferred phlogiston to the air. When the air was full of phlogiston, it wouldn't accept any more and nothing more would burn in it. Rutherford, therefore, called the gas he had ended with, "phlogisticated air."

A few years later, however, Rutherford's gas came to be called "nitrogen" (NY-troh-jen). This was from Greek words meaning "nitre-producer," because it was found that the gas could be produced from a mineral called "nitre."

In 1774 another gas was discovered by the English chemist Joseph Priestley (1733–1804). When Priestley formed the new gas and wanted to study it, he led the gas through a glass tube into a dish of mercury and allowed the gas to bubble up into an upended container of mercury, whose mouth was held under the surface of the mercury in the dish. The new gas

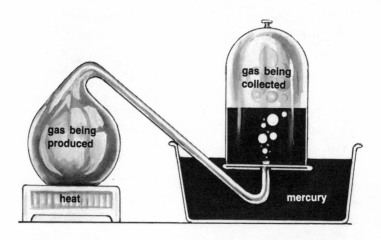

forced the mercury out of the upended container into the dish. He then put a glass lid over the container's opening, took it out of the dish of mercury, and turned it rightside up.

In this way the gas never mixed with air, so its properties could be studied with greater ease. The gas also never came in contact with water, in which some gases dissolved.

These results got Priestley interested in mercury, though, and he found that when mercury was heated, a rust-red powder formed on its surface. He collected some of this powder, heated it, and found that it broke down into shiny little drops of mercury again. In the process, a gas was given off.

Priestley collected a container of this new gas and studied its properties. He found that things burned *more easily* in the new gas than they did in air. He took a splinter of wood, set one end on fire, and blew it out so that the ending just glowed red-hot, but didn't actually show a flame. When he pushed the glowing wood splinter into the new gas, it promptly burst into flame.

Priestley thought that air must have a little phlogiston in it, but not much, which was why wood burned in it. This new gas, he thought, must be air from which even that little bit of phlogiston was removed, so that wood burned in it more easily and rapidly than in ordinary air. He called the gas "dephlogisticated air."

Soon, however, Priestley's gas received the name of "oxygen" (OK-sih-jen), from Greek words meaning "acid-producer." This was because chemists came to think that acids always contained oxygen atoms in their molecules. As it happened, this proved to be wrong, but by that time it was too late to change the name again.

In 1766, even before nitrogen and oxygen were discovered, the English chemist Henry Cavendish (1731–1810) had found that when acids were added to certain metals, the metals were eaten away, and a gas was formed. Cavendish collected the gas and studied it.

He found it was very light. Cavendish was the first to compare the densities of various gases; that is, he tried to find out how much a given volume of different gases weighed. He found, for instance, that the air in a container of a certain size might weigh fourteen ounces. If he filled that container with his new gas, that quantity of the gas weighed only one ounce. His new gas was only one fourteenth as dense as air. It was the lightest of all the gases Cavendish studied, and it is the lightest known gas even today.

In addition, it turned out that the new gas burned very easily; and, in fact, it exploded when heated. Cavendish called it "fire air" and wondered if it might be phlogiston itself. When Cavendish's gas burned, it produced droplets of liquid that turned out to be water. Therefore, the gas came to be called "hydrogen" (HY-droh-jen) from the Greek words meaning "water-producer."

In 1774, the French chemist Antoine Laurent Lavoisier (la-vwah-ZYAY, 1743–1794) had been studying combustion for quite a while. He found that when he heated objects in closed containers so that they burned or, in the case of metals, rusted, there was no change in the weight of the container with its load of chemicals. He also found that the rusted metals and the ash of some of the things that burned were heavier than the original material.

If the metals had gained weight and the whole container was the same weight as before, then something else in the container must have lost weight to balance the gain. The only other thing in the container was air, so the air must have lost weight. Some of it must be gone.

Lavoisier proved this was so, for when he opened the container, air rushed in to replace the portion of the air that had been lost. What's more, if he let metal rust in a container of air that was turned upside down in a pan of water, as the metal rusted, water rose higher in the container to replace the air that was used up. In the end, the water rose to replace about one-fifth of the air.

Lavoisier decided that the phlogiston theory was all wrong. Air didn't change because phlogiston was added or taken away. In fact, phlogiston did not exist. Instead, air was not an element. It was a mixture of two entirely different gases, each of which *was* an element. Air was four-fifths nitrogen and one-fifth oxygen.

Lavoisier argued that when something burned or rusted, it combined with the oxygen and became heavier. The oxygen disappeared and only the nitrogen was left behind, and nothing would burn in nitrogen. When iron rusted, it combined with oxygen and the rust could be called "iron oxide." When mercury was heated, it combined with oxygen to produce the brick-red "mercuric oxide," and when mercuric oxide was heated, it broke up into mercury and oxygen again. In the pure oxygen obtained from mercuric oxide, things burned more rapidly than in air, which was only one-fifth oxygen.

In this way, Rutherford's experiment and Priestley's experiment were explained without any need for talk about phlogiston.

The molecules present in wood and in candles contain carbon atoms. (Coal is an example of something that is made up almost entirely of carbon atoms.) When carbon atoms combine with oxygen, carbon dioxide is formed and this, unlike most oxides, is a gas and vanishes into the air. That is why the ash left by wood is much lighter than the wood itself, and why the wax in a candle seems to disappear altogether.

This understanding of combustion, together with the atomic theory that followed twenty-five years later, founded modern chemistry.

Lavoisier in his laboratory

3 Molecules and Heights

THANKS TO LAVOISIER, people found out what air really was. Nowadays, we know that air is 78 percent nitrogen and 21 percent oxygen (very nearly 4/5 and 1/5, as Lavoisier had calculated). Notice, though, that 78 plus 21 is equal to 99. What is the remaining 1 percent of the air made of?

There is water vapor in the air usually, but that doesn't count. The water vapor is removed (and so is dust) before the air is studied, and it is dry, pure air that is 78 percent nitrogen and 21 percent oxygen. There is also a little carbon dioxide in the air, but the amount of that gas that is present is far less than 1 percent.

The first to realize that there was something present in air besides oxygen and nitrogen was Cavendish, the discoverer of hydrogen.

In 1785, he passed electric sparks through a quantity of air. The electric sparks contained so much energy that they forced nitrogen atoms to combine with oxygen atoms to form "nitrogen oxide." (Ordinary heat doesn't have enough energy to produce that combination, or a forest fire would be enough to destroy the atmosphere in its present form.)

The molecules of nitrogen oxide can be dissolved in water and removed, and in this way, all the oxygen was finally used up. There was still nitrogen left, however. Cavendish added more oxygen and combined that with nitrogen and then added still more oxygen.

Eventually, Cavendish thought, he would be left with no gas at all, either nitrogen or oxygen, and he would have proved that air was made up of nitrogen and oxygen *only*. Other substances, like carbon dioxide, would be present in only tiny, or "trace," quantities.

No matter what Cavendish did, however, he was always left over with a small quantity of gas, about 1 percent of the whole, that would not combine with oxygen even under the push of the electric spark. That small quantity was neither oxygen nor nitrogen, but it was part of the air. Cavendish reported this, but no one paid much attention, and the matter of the missing 1 percent was forgotten for a whole century.

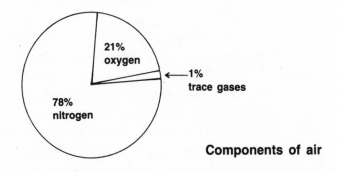

Components of air

There were advances in other directions, though. In 1811, an Italian scientist, Amedeo Avogadro (ah-voh-GAH-droh, 1776–1856), studied what was known about gases and made a suggestion. He said that in order to make sense out of gases, a given volume of any gas had to have the same number of particles in it. The particles might be single atoms or they might be molecules. By studying the density of the gases, the weight of the particles could then be worked out.

For instance, people had an idea of the weight of the oxygen atom as compared to other atoms. If oxygen gas were made up of single atoms, then it ought to have a certain density. Actually oxygen has twice that density. The decision then must be that each particle of oxygen is a molecule that is made up of *two* oxygen atoms. Chemists therefore write the oxygen molecule as "O_2" for short. In the same way, nitrogen and hydrogen turned out to be made up of molecules of two atoms each, so that they can be written "N_2" and "H_2."

This wasn't decided the minute Avogadro made his suggestion, of course. Scientists are human beings. It sometimes takes them quite a while to accept something new.

In 1860, the chemists of Europe got together in an international meeting to try to straighten out some of the confusions in chemical thinking at the time. One person attending was the Italian chemist Stanislao Cannizzaro (kahn-need-DZAH-roh, 1826–1910). He had come across Avogadro's suggestion two years before, and he realized that it would clear up at least some of the confusion chemists had about how many atoms there were in particular molecules. He pre-

Montgolfier's hot-air balloon launched June 3, 1783

sented it to the meeting and convinced most of the chemists there.

That meant that by 1860, chemists finally had the chemical makeup of air completely worked out—or, at least, they had 99 percent of it completely worked out.

Of course, scientists were working mainly with the air that was near the ground, the air they could reach. It seemed to make sense to suppose that the air farther up would be just like the air lower down, at least as far as the natures of the different gases present. Could one be sure, however?

One way of studying the air higher up would be to climb a mountain as Pascal's brother-in-law did. Climbing mountains, however, is difficult and dangerous work. What's more, the mountains in Europe are not terribly high. There are higher mountains far away in South America and Asia, but they are terribly difficult to climb and even the highest mountain in the world is only five-and-a-half miles high.

In 1783, however, two French inventors, Joseph Michel Montgolfier (mohn-gohl-FYAY, 1740–1810) and his brother Jacques Étienne Montgolfier (1745–1799), invented the balloon. The balloon is a large bag filled with a gas that is lighter than air so that it rises upward, as wood would rise upward if it were released under water.

Montgolfier's first balloon, launched on June 3, 1783, used hot air, but the French scientist Jacques Alexandre Charles (SHAHRL, 1746–1823) at once suggested that hydrogen should be used, and a hydrogen balloon was sent up on August 27, 1783.

At once ballooning was very popular in Europe. Female aeronauts became a novelty. Jeanne Labrosse was the first woman to pilot a balloon herself. Most of the people interested in it were just thinking of the thrills and excitement. Some, however, thought of scientific knowledge. It was much easier and faster to go up in a balloon than up the side of a mountain.

In 1784, an American doctor, John Jeffries (1745–1810), went up in a balloon in London, taking with him a barometer and devices with which to collect samples of air from high up. It was the first scientific investigation by balloon.

Jeffries didn't go up very high, but in 1804, the French chemist Joseph Louis Gay-Lussac (GAY-lyoo-SAK, 1778–1850), rose nearly four-and-one-half miles in a balloon. This was a mile higher than any mountain peak in Europe. Gay-Lussac brought down air from this height and found it had the same composition as the air near Earth's surface.

The air was thin, though, at that height. Gay-Lussac, standing in an open gondola under the balloon, didn't find it easy to breathe. It also got colder as one went higher, for the thin air didn't hold much heat. The cold made it uncomfortable, too.

In 1875, three men went up in a balloon and set a new record for height, for they rose six miles. The trouble was that two died as a result, and only one, Gaston Tissandier (tis-an-DYAY, 1843–1899), came back alive. After that, there were no further attempts to go up to a great height in open gondolas.

Beginning in 1892, unmanned balloons were sent up. They carried thermometers, barometers, and other instruments which recorded conditions at various heights. When the balloons came back, the instruments could be recovered and studied.

**Jacques Charles hydrogen balloon
sent up August 27, 1783**

A French scientist, Leon Philippe Teisserenc de Bort (tes-RAHN-duh-BAWR, 1855–1913), conducted many of these unmanned balloon studies. He found that the air grew colder as the balloons went higher until a temperature of 55 degrees below zero, Celsius (−55 C) was reached. That is equal to 67 degrees below zero, Fahrenheit (−67 F), and that is as cold as a Siberian winter.

When the balloons went still higher, however, it turned out that the temperature didn't drop any further, but stayed steady.

In 1902, Teisserenc de Bort suggested that the atmosphere had two main regions. The lower one possessed all the weather. It contained the clouds, the winds, the rain, snow, and so on. Teisserenc de Bort called it the "troposphere" (TROH-poh-sfeer), which comes from the Greek words meaning "the sphere of change." He believed that the troposphere extended up to ten miles above the surface of the equator. As one moved away from the equator, however, the top of the troposphere moved lower. At the poles, the troposphere was only five miles high.

The top of the troposphere is where the temperature stops dropping. Teisserenc de Bort felt that in the region above the troposphere, where there was no wind or weather, the thin air lay in quiet layers. Therefore, he called that region the "stratosphere" (STRAT-oh-sfeer), which comes from the Greek words meaning "the sphere of layers."

Fashionable Parisians watch the first woman, Jeanne Labrosse, pilot a balloon herself in 1798.

4 Noble Gases and Ions

MEANWHILE, THE QUESTION of the nature of that missing 1 percent of the atmosphere came up again.

The English scientist John William Strutt Lord Rayleigh (RAY-lee, 1842–1919) was studying nitrogen very carefully from 1882 on. He wanted to know how much nitrogen atoms weighed compared to other kinds of atoms. He collected the nitrogen that he studied in two chief ways: first, from the air by removing all the oxygen, water vapor, carbon dioxide, dust and so on; secondly, from various kinds of minerals.

He found that the nitrogen atoms from the minerals all had the same weight, regardless of which minerals he got it from. The nitrogen from the air, however, had atoms that weighed a little bit more than the nitrogen from the minerals did. Rayleigh couldn't figure out what was wrong and when he published his results, he asked if any other scientists had ideas about it.

A Scottish chemist, Sir William Ramsay (RAM-zee, 1852–1916), asked permission to tackle the problem. He remembered that Cavendish had discovered a little bubble of air that wouldn't combine with any-thing. What if that was an unknown gas with atoms heavier than those of nitrogen? Nitrogen from miner-als would be just nitrogen and nothing else, but nitrogen from air would have a few of those heavy atoms and, on the average, the nitrogen atoms from air would then seem a little heavier than they should be.

By this time, chemists had the "spectroscope" (SPEK-troh-skope), an instrument that could be used to identify atoms and molecules. If gas is heated it gives off light. The light consists of tiny waves. Each kind of atom or molecule gives off its own particular lightwaves of different length. From the "wave-lengths" you can identify the atom or molecule, just as you can identify a human being from his fingerprints.

Ramsay repeated Cavendish's experiment and found that that last little bubble of air emitted wave-lengths different from nitrogen. In fact, they were different from any element that was then known. In 1895, Ramsay was sure he had a new element, and he and Rayleigh named it "argon" (AHR-gon) from the Greek word meaning "inert" or "lazy," because it wouldn't combine with anything else. The argon atoms wouldn't even combine with each other so that argon gas was made up of single atoms. Even so, a single argon atom is much heavier than the combina-tion of two nitrogen atoms forming the nitrogen molecule.

This meant that pure, dry air is made up of 78 percent nitrogen, 21 percent oxygen, and 1 percent argon. Anything else is present only in traces.

In Ramsay's day, chemists had learned a lot about

Sir William Ramsay

the various elements. They knew that if argon existed, there must also be several other similar elements with atoms that did not combine with anything else. Ramsay began to search for them.

The same year that the discovery of argon was announced, Ramsay heard that there was a mineral that gave off a gas when heated, a gas that was reported to be nitrogen. Was it really?

Ramsay got a sample of the gas, heated it, and studied the wavelengths of the light it gave off. It certainly was not nitrogen. It wasn't argon, either.

To Ramsay's surprise, the wavelengths were the same as those reported in sunlight back in 1868 by the French astronomer Pierre Jules César Janssen (zhahn-SEN, 1824–1907). Janssen thought the lines represented an unknown element found in the Sun, and it was therefore named "helium" (HEE-lee-um) from the Greek word for "sun." And now Ramsay had found helium on Earth.

Ramsay went on to prepare a considerable quantity of argon and to study it very carefully to see if there were small quantities of other, similar gases mixed with it. In 1898, he found three more: "neon" (NEE-on), from the Greek word for "new"; "krypton" (KRIP-ton), from the Greek word for "hidden"; and "xenon" (ZEE-non), from the Greek word for "stranger."

These three, with argon and helium, are lumped together as "inert gases" or "noble gases." They are all present in the atmosphere, but all except argon are present in tiny quantities. Only 1/50,000 of the atmosphere is neon. Helium, krypton, and xenon are present in even smaller amounts. Also present in small amounts are carbon dioxide, hydrogen, and methane. Methane is made up of molecules containing a carbon atom and four hydrogen atoms (CH_4).

It is difficult to get sizable quantities of the inert gases out of air, or it would be if we had to work with ordinary air. About the time Ramsay was beginning his work, though, something new was being done with air.

At the beginning of the 1800s, air remained a gas no matter how much cold it was exposed to. As the years progressed, however, scientists learned how to reach lower and lower temperatures so that gas after gas was made liquid, or "liquefied."

Finally, in 1877, a French scientist, Louis Paul Cailletet (ka-yuh-TAY, 1832–1913), managed to reach a temperature so low that even oxygen and nitrogen were liquefied. Oxygen turns liquid at $-183°C$ ($-297°F$), and nitrogen turns liquid at $-194°C$ ($-320°F$). Once those two gases were liquefied, it was possible to liquefy air but, at first, only in tiny quantities.

A German chemist, Karl Linde (LIN-duh, 1842–1934), tackled the matter and, in 1895, worked out a way to form "liquid air" in large quantities and rather cheaply. Liquid air is much denser than ordinary gaseous air, so that a gallon of liquid air contains far more molecules of all the substances making it up than a gallon of gaseous air. Chemists could make use of liquid air to get out large quantities of pure oxygen or pure nitrogen, or sizable amounts of the individual noble gases—even xenon, the rarest of them.

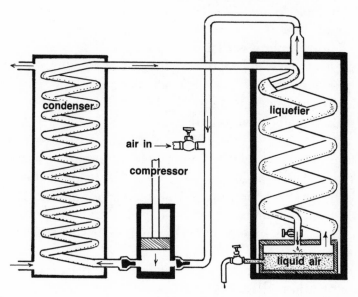

Apparatus for liquefying air

Auguste Piccard and his assistant wearing protection for the head on their ascent in May 1931

By the end of the 1800s, then, the composition of the air was known completely, but scientists still looked longingly to the heights. Human beings hadn't gone more than six miles high. Balloons had, but not human beings.

The trouble was that the high air was so thin—but did they have to breathe it? Instead of standing in an open basket, why couldn't a balloon carry a sealed cabin with normal dense air in it?

Eventually, that was done. A Swiss scientist, Auguste Piccard (pee-KAHR, 1884–1962), constructed large balloons, with comfortable aluminum cabins underneath. Beginning in 1931, he made balloon flights that carried him as much as eleven miles high. He used helium to lift the balloon. Helium is not quite as light as hydrogen, but it is much safer since it can't possibly burn or explode.

Later on, balloons were made out of plastic materials rather than silk and carried men more than twenty miles high. Unmanned balloons rose over thirty miles.

The higher flights showed that the temperature didn't remain constant as one rose through the stratosphere. It started rising. The stratosphere came to an end at a height of 30 miles. Above that lay the "upper atmosphere."

Only 2 percent of the weight of the atmosphere lies above a height of twenty miles, but that's enough to produce some interesting effects.

For instance, it is quite common to see "meteors" (MEE-tee-awrz), also called "shooting stars," in the night sky. They are bits of matter, mostly quite small, that fly through outer space and happen to collide with the Earth. As they rush through the upper atmosphere, they force the molecules together. This turns the energy of their motion into heat and they begin to glow brightly and melt. The air may be very thin at great heights, but there is enough of it to heat up the meteor and make it visible even at heights of from sixty to eighty miles.

Gondola of Piccard's balloon being retrieved from Bavarian Alps landing site

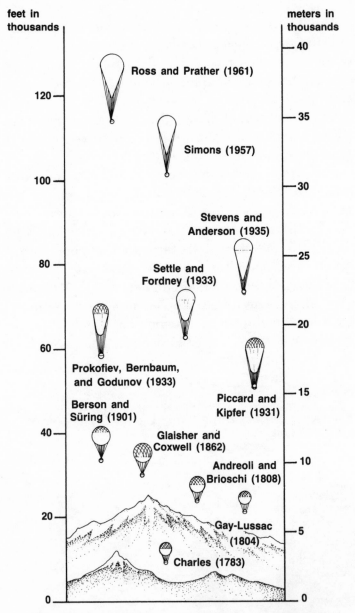

feet in thousands

meters in thousands

Ross and Prather (1961)

Simons (1957)

Stevens and Anderson (1935)

Settle and Fordney (1933)

Prokofiev, Bernbaum, and Godunov (1933)

Piccard and Kipfer (1931)

Berson and Süring (1901)

Glaisher and Coxwell (1862)

Andreoli and Brioschi (1808)

Gay-Lussac (1804)

Charles (1783)

Altitudes reached by two centuries of aeronauts

Then, too, there are tiny particles hurled out of the Sun at great speeds, particles even smaller than atoms. These particles make up the "solar wind." The particles possess an electric charge and a great deal of energy. They speed away from the Sun in all directions and some of them strike the Earth. In doing so, they penetrate the Earth's upper atmosphere and smash those atoms and molecules they happen to hit.

The smashed atoms and molecules also carry an electric charge and are called "ions" (EYE-onz). They are more energetic than normal, intact atoms.

Naturally, the solar wind only hits the daylight side of the Earth. The night side is protected by the bulk of the planet. The smashed atoms have a chance to recover the missing parts of themselves and to lose the additional energy they gained. The energy they lose makes its appearance in the form of light.

The solar wind is forced to curve by the Earth's magnetism so that is mostly hits near the poles. That is where most of the light given off by the smashed atoms is to be seen. This light is called the "aurora" (aw-RAW-ruh) and is a feature of the polar night.

There is enough air one hundred miles above the Earth's surface to produce an easily visible aurora. Sometimes an aurora can be seen at a height of six hundred miles.

Eventually, in the 1950s, scientists learned how to send rockets to great heights—even beyond the atmosphere altogether. In this way, it was discovered that there were enough atoms and molecules of gas to affect rocket flight even at heights of twelve hundred miles. At these great heights, most of the gas is made up of helium atoms, hydrogen atoms, and hydrogen molecules, the lightest of all gases to be found in the earth's atmosphere—or anywhere else.

In 1901, the Italian electrical engineer Guglielmo Marconi (mahr-KOH-nee, 1874–1937) sent radio waves across the Atlantic Ocean from England to Newfoundland. This was puzzling, for radio waves could only travel in straight lines. To go from England to Newfoundland, however, the radio waves had to curve around the bulge of the spherical Earth. How could that happen?

In 1902, the British-American electrical engineer Arthur Edwin Kennelly (1861–1939) argued that radio waves would be reflected by air containing quantities of ions. He suggested that there was a region in the upper atmosphere that was rich in ions. Radio waves would bounce from the ions to the ground, back to the ions, and so forth. In that way, they would travel in zigzagging straight lines around the bulge of the Earth.

An English electrical engineer, Oliver Heaviside (HEV-ih-side, 1850–1925), made the same suggestion at about the same time, so people spoke of the "Kennelly-Heaviside layer."

In 1924, the English scientist Edward Victor Appleton (1892–1965), sent radio waves up into the air and was able to show that they really did bounce back. The Kennelly-Heaviside layer was about seventy miles high, and beyond it lay other layers up to one hundred and fifty miles high. The Scottish scientist Robert Alexander Watson-Watt (1892–1937) suggested that the portion of the atmosphere that was rich in ions, from sixty to one hundred and fifty miles up, be called the "ionosphere" (eye-ON-oh-sfeer).

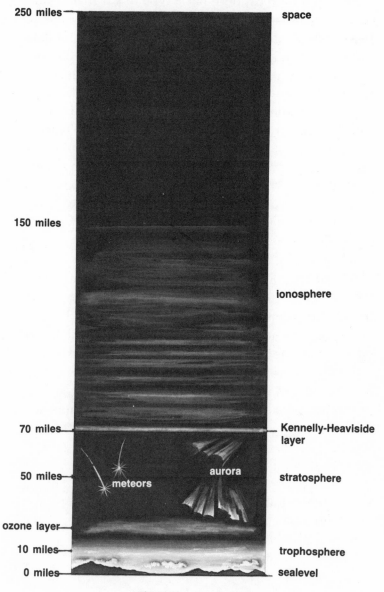

250 miles — space

150 miles

ionosphere

70 miles — Kennelly-Heaviside layer

aurora

50 miles — stratosphere

meteors

ozone layer —

10 miles — trophosphere

0 miles — sealevel

Earth's atmosphere

The upper atmosphere has a type of gas that is very rare lower down. The history of that gas goes back to 1840, when the German-Swiss chemist Christian Friedrich Schönbein (SHOIN-bine, 1799–1868) became curious about a peculiar smell around electrical equipment. He found it was due to a gas which he isolated, studied, and named "ozone" (OH-zone), which comes from the Greek word meaning "smell."

Eventually, ozone was found to be a form of oxygen, but one with three oxygen atoms (O_3) in its molecule instead of only two. Ozone contains more energy than oxygen and forms from oxygen only in the presence of a good supply of energy, such as that around electrical equipment. When the energy is removed, ozone quickly breaks down to oxygen again.

In 1913, a French scientist, Charles Fabry (fah-BREE, 1867–1945), showed that there was ozone in the upper atmosphere. It forms from oxygen through the energetic action of sunlight. The sunlight forms more ozone as fast as the molecules break down.

The ozone region in the atmosphere, at the height of about fifteen miles, is called the "ozonosphere" (oh-ZOH-noh-sfeer). The ozonosphere is very important to us. It absorbs the very energetic ultra-violet light of the sun. If that light could pass through the ozonosphere, it would have no trouble passing through the oxygen and nitrogen of the lower atmosphere. Then it would strike Earth's surface and the living things on it (including us) and do a great deal of damage. It is the ozone in the stratosphere that protects us.

Modern balloon

5 Other Worlds

THE ATOMS AND molecules in solid substances hold together tightly, but it is different with gases. The molecules of gases don't hold together at all, but spread apart from each other as widely as they can. The gases in Earth's atmosphere would spread apart and disappear into outer space, except that they are held to the ground by the Earth's gravitational pull.

The smaller a planet, the less gravitational pull it has. The Moon, for instance, has only one-sixth the gravitational pull of the earth at its surface. The Moon's gravitational pull is not enough to hold an atmosphere. The Moon is, therefore, airless. So are all astronomical objects that are smaller than the Moon.

The hotter a planet is, the more rapidly gas molecules move about, and the harder it is for gravitational pull to hold them. Take Mercury and Mars, for instance. They are each smaller than Earth, and each has a gravitational pull on its surface about two-fifths that of Earth. Mercury, which is the planet closest to the Sun, is very hot, and its gravitational pull is too small to be able to hold an atmosphere at that temperature. It is as airless as the Moon, therefore.

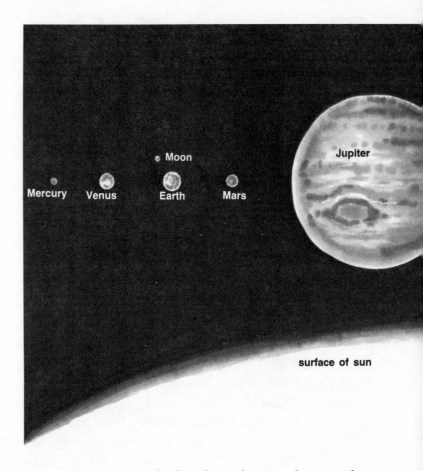

Mercury Venus Moon Earth Mars Jupiter

surface of sun

Mars, however, is farther from the Sun than Earth is and is colder than Antarctica. Its gravitational pull therefore manages to hold on to an atmosphere, but a very thin one; one that is only about 1/100 as dense as Earth's atmosphere.

Just because another planet has an atmosphere doesn't mean that that atmosphere contains the same gases ours does. It is strange, for instance, for any

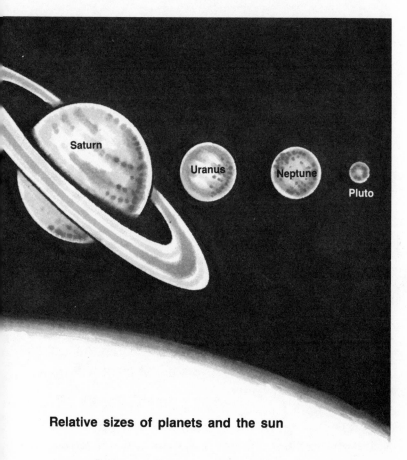

Relative sizes of planets and the sun

atmosphere to have a great deal of oxygen in it. Oxygen is an active gas that combines easily with other substances. Ordinarily, it would undergo such combination and slowly disappear from the atmosphere, if it ever got into it in the first place.

The reason there is oxygen in our atmosphere is that green plants use the energy of sunlight to build their structure out of carbon dioxide and water. In the

Green plants use the energy of sunlight to produce carbohydrates from carbon dioxide and water

In the process they give off oxygen

Animals breathe the air, combining oxygen with the food to form carbon dioxide and water

Oxygen cycle

process they give off oxygen. Animals breathe the air, combining the oxygen with sugars in the plant to form carbon dioxide and water.

This sets up a balance. The plants form oxygen as fast as it is used up by animals and in other ways. The result is that oxygen remains in Earth's atmosphere for all the hundreds of millions of years that plants have been forming it.

Before plants developed ways of making use of carbon dioxide and forming oxygen, there was probably no oxygen in Earth's atmosphere. There was carbon dioxide instead. If green plants hadn't come into existence, Earth's atmosphere would have consisted of carbon dioxide and nitrogen to this very day.

In fact, as we know from our rocket probes in the 1970s, Mars's thin atmosphere is made up of carbon dioxide and nitrogen. It is one way we can tell that it can't possibly have any kind of life similar to ours, except of the simplest varieties.

Venus is a planet that is almost as large as Earth, and one that has almost as much gravitational pull. It has a dense atmosphere of carbon dioxide and nitrogen.

Venus is closer to the Sun than Earth is, and is therefore hotter. On Earth, a great deal of carbon dioxide is combined with minerals to form "carbonates" (KAHR-buh-nates). On Venus, the greater heat breaks down any carbonates that exist and releases carbon dioxide gas into the atmosphere.

Dense clouds around Venus

Carbon dioxide holds heat, so the more carbon dioxide in the atmosphere, the hotter Venus gets. As Venus gets hotter, still more carbonates break down. In the end, Venus developed an atmosphere nearly a hundred times as dense as Earth's and one that is very rich in carbon dioxide. Such an atmosphere holds so much heat that Venus is the hottest planet in the solar system. It is even hotter than Mercury, which is closer to the Sun than Venus is, but which has no atmosphere to hold the heat.

Moons of Saturn

The smaller an atom or molecule is, the faster it moves at a particular temperature, and the harder it is for a gravitational pull to hang on to it. The smallest atoms are those of hydrogen and helium.

The material out of which the Earth and the other planets were originally formed was almost all hydrogen and helium. Earth and the nearby planets were formed fairly close to the Sun, so they were too hot to hang on to hydrogen and helium. They were formed out of the small quantity of heavier atoms and molecules that existed. That's why Earth, Mars, Venus, Mercury, and the Moon are as small as they are.

Farther out from the Sun, it was cooler and the forming planets could hold on to hydrogen and helium. That made them larger and gave them a greater gravitational pull so they could hold on to hydrogen and helium all the better. For that reason, Jupiter, Saturn, Uranus, and Neptune came to be giant planets. The atmospheres of the giant planets are deep and dense and are mostly hydrogen and helium.

The satellites of the giant planets are too small to have atmospheres even in the frigid cold of the outer reaches of the solar system. There is one exception and that is Titan, the largest satellite of the planet Saturn. It is just large enough and cold enough to hang on to an atmosphere.

Titan's atmosphere was discovered in 1948 by the Dutch-American astronomer Gerard Peter Kuiper (KOY-per, 1905–1973). He studied its light by spectroscope and detected methane. In 1983, a rocket probe flashed past Saturn and found that Titan's atmosphere was mostly nitrogen, an element that doesn't show up well in the spectroscope.

As far as we now know, then, there are, in our solar system, seven planets and one satellite that have atmospheres.

Four planets (Jupiter, Saturn, Uranus, and Neptune) have atmospheres that are mostly hydrogen and helium.

Two planets (Venus and Mars) have atmospheres that are mostly carbon dioxide and nitrogen.

One satellite (Titan) has an atmosphere that is mostly nitrogen and methane.

One planet (Earth) has an atmosphere that is mostly nitrogen and oxygen.

Of all the planets we know, only Earth has oxygen in its atmosphere, and that makes it the only one on which human beings can live easily.

Peaceable Kingdom, a painting by Edward Hicks in 1830

Index